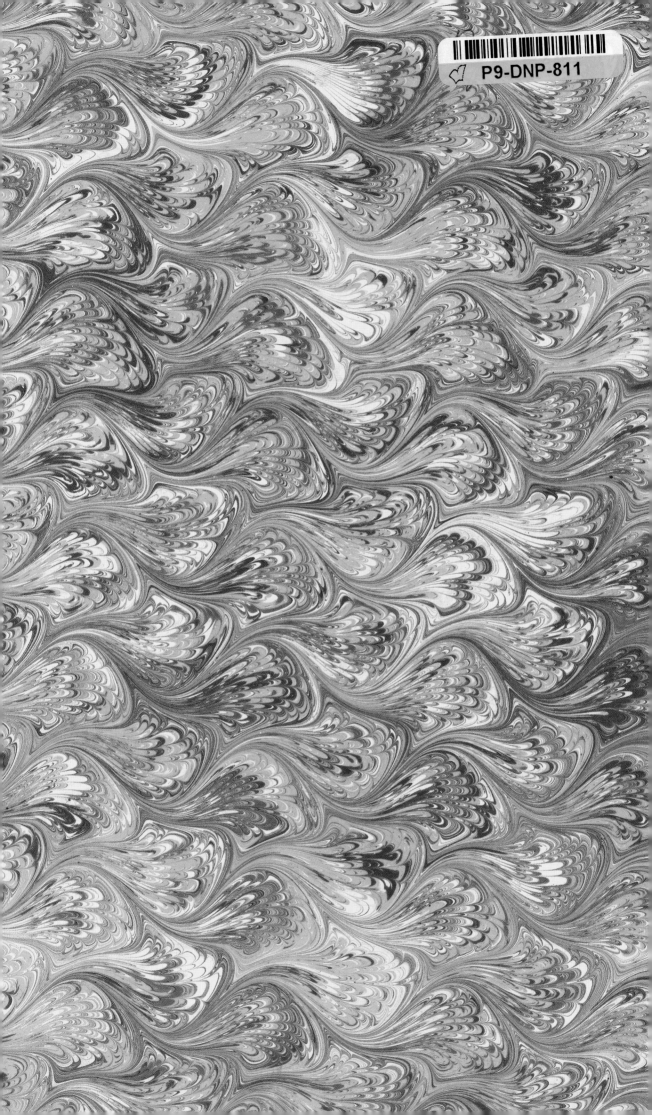

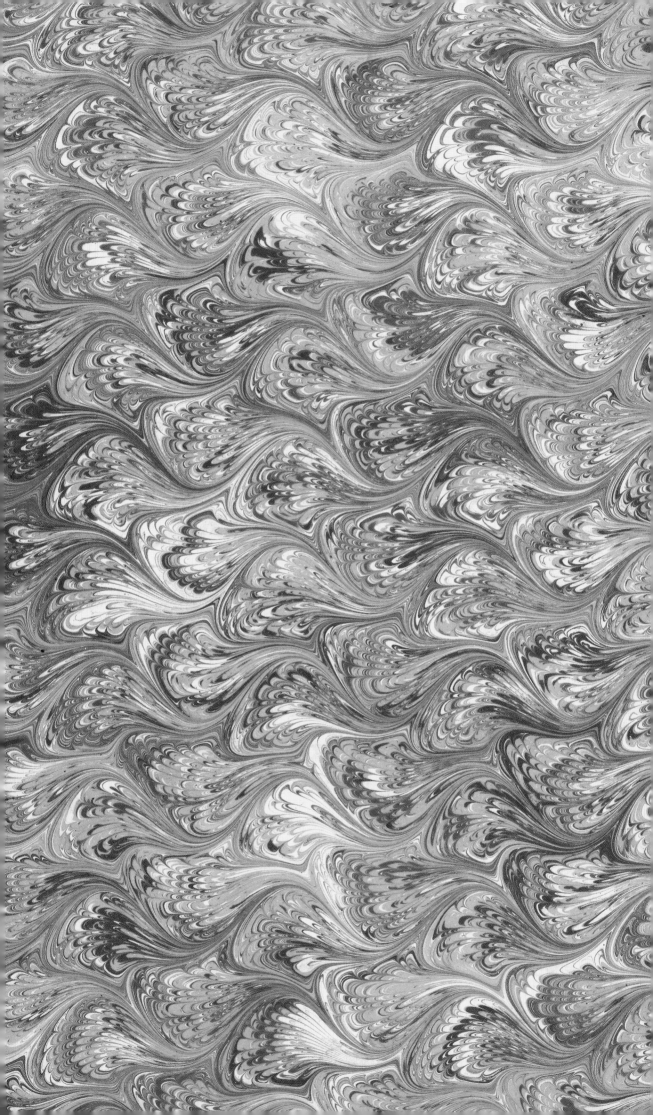

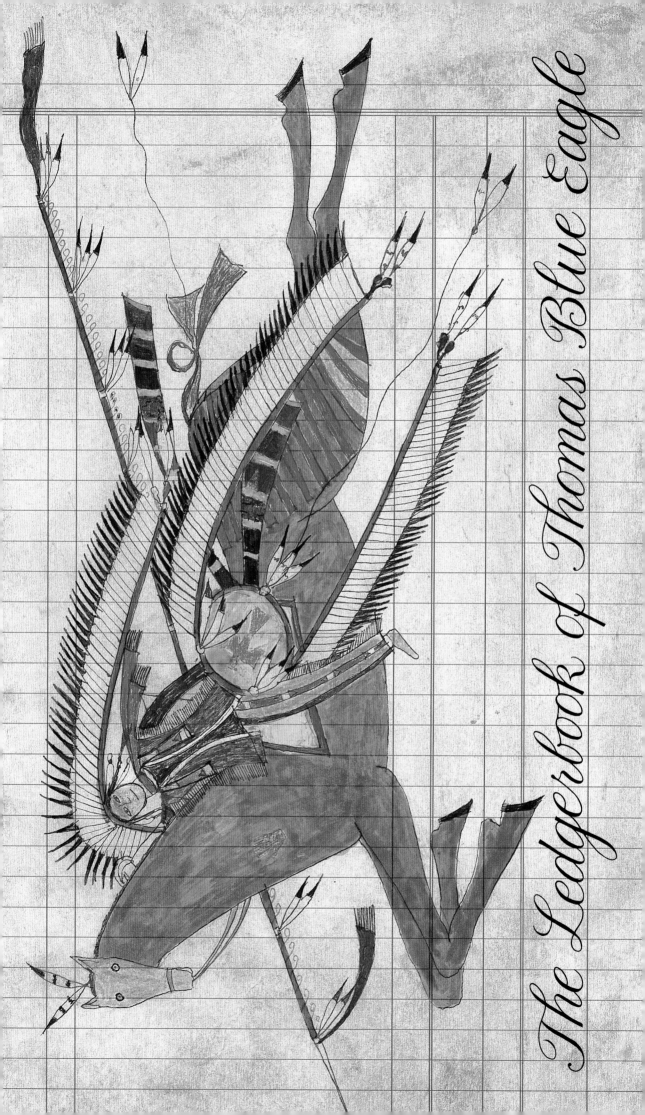

The Ledgerbook of Thomas Blue Eagle

I was born in the Moon When Ponies Shed Their Shaggy Hair.

I was horseback before I could walk. When I was eight winters,

my father, called Iron Arm, gave me my own beautiful pony.

My pony was strong and proud, and at first we had many

arguments. I painted him with different earth colors on each

side and called him Two Painted Horse. Often I tied up his

tail as if for war and gave him bird feathers to wear in his mane.

Two Painted Horse was my very best friend.

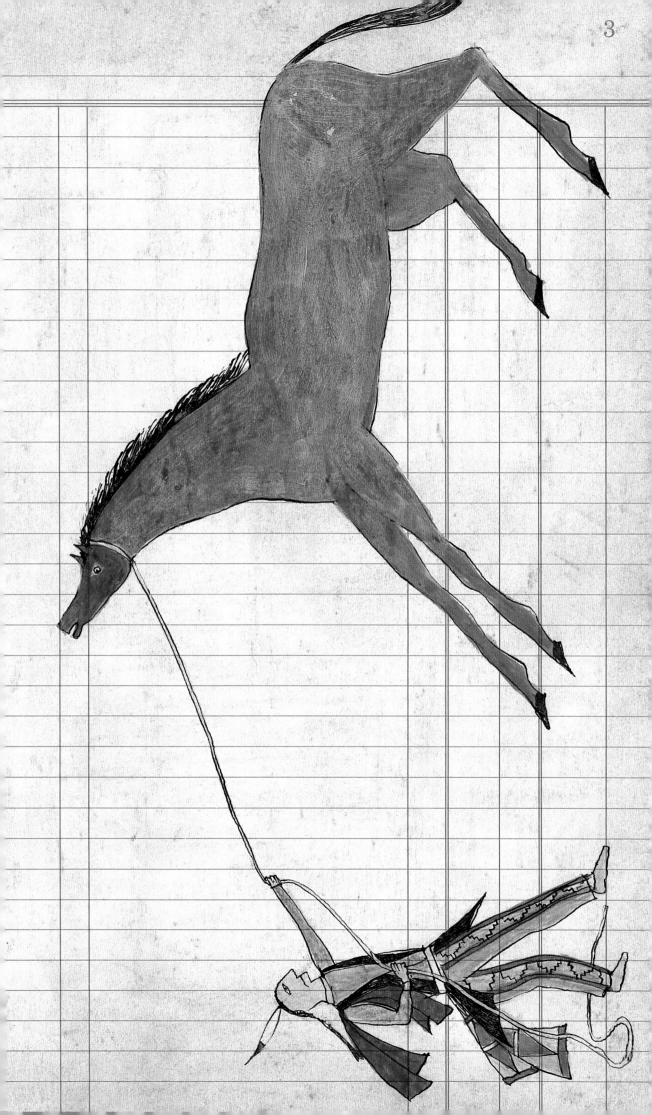

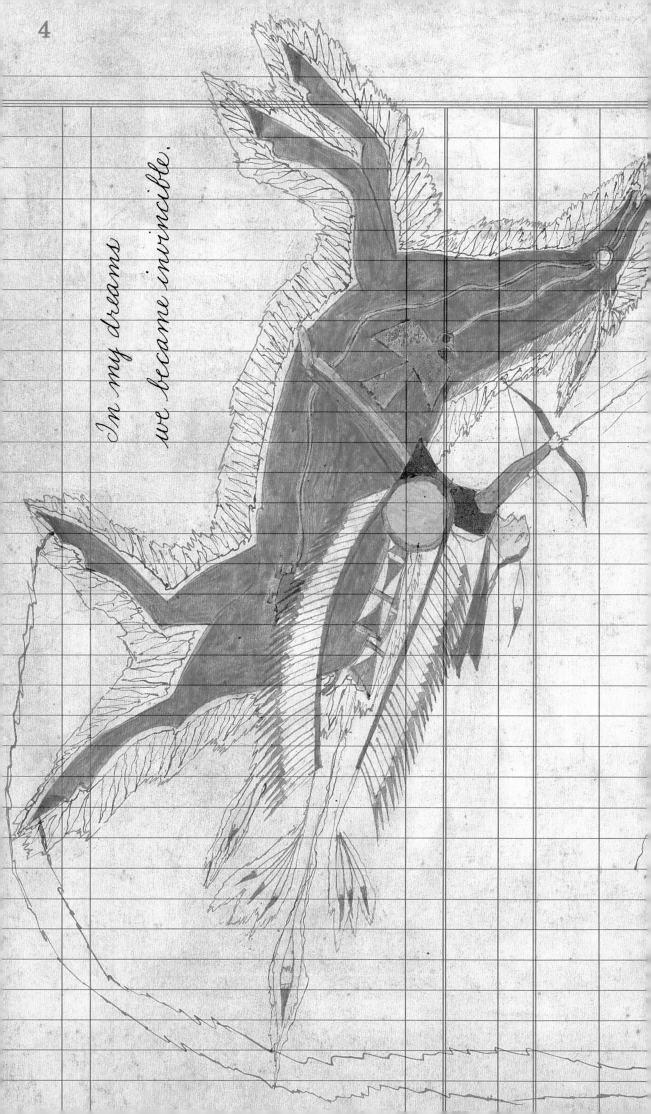

*In my dreams
we became invincible.*

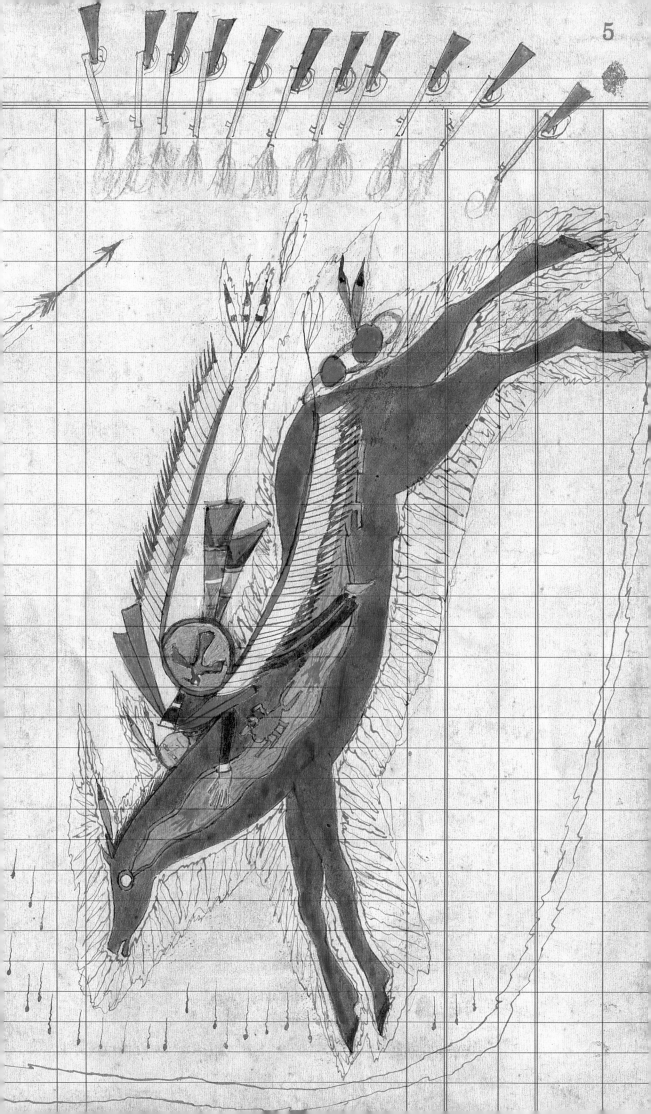

My father taught me to be brave. He said it is far more brave to touch an enemy or take his horse than to kill him. My father also taught me to shoot my bow. He made me blunt headed arrows so that I did not hurt myself. Soon I was able to hit far away targets while racing about on Two Painted Horse.

But the greatest coup I could count would be to touch an enemy with my bow, not to hit him with my arrows. All our warriors painted pictures of their brave deeds or marked them on coup sticks.

We were the people of the buffalo. They gave us our tipis, our clothes, our meat, our robes, tools, shields, bowstrings, sewing thread, and runners for our winter sleds.

We lived side by side with the buffalo. Their life gave us life, and we hunted them only for what we needed. We had many ceremonies to thank the buffalo and honor its spirit. Red Feather,

our holy man, warned us that one day a strange pale tribe would come and make a fence around us and then the buffalo would run back into the earth, taking our way of life with them.

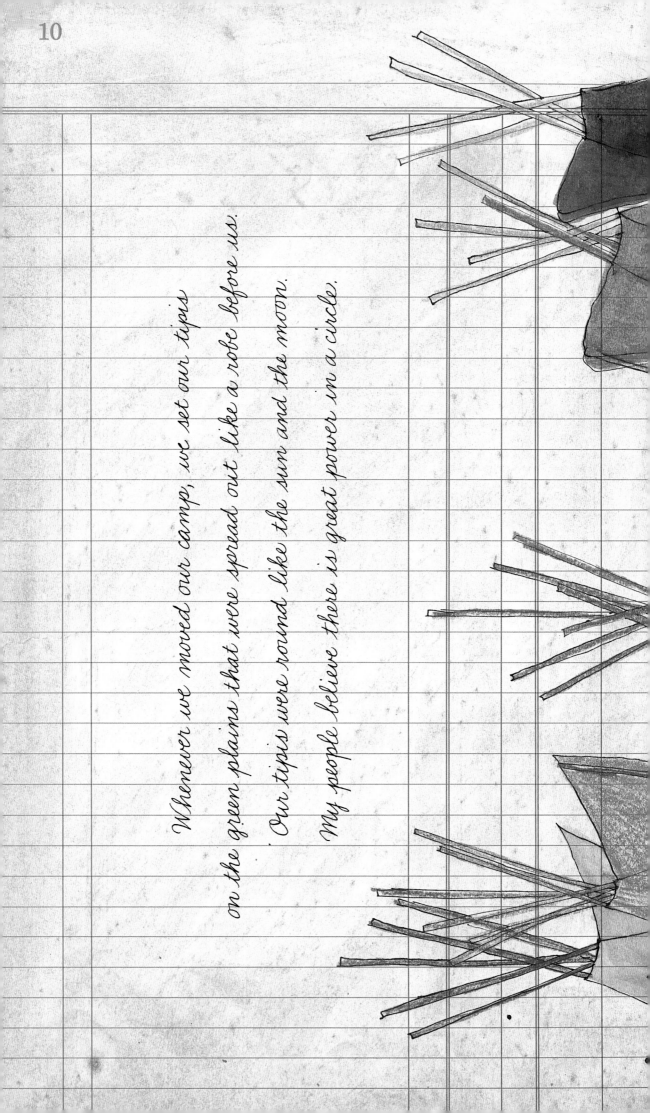

Whenever we moved our camp, we set our tipis
on the green plains that were spread out like a robe before us.
Our tipis were round like the sun and the moon.
My people believe there is great power in a circle.

12

My people had no books with words, but we had picture writing. Our storytellers would speak our history around the council fire, and each year Red Feather would paint that winter's count of our hunts and battles and sacred events on a buffalo hide. We made our paints from baked earth and crushed berries and our brushes from buffalo bones and sharpened sticks. For paint pots we used turtle shells. All these gifts came from our Mother Earth. Sometimes we traded for other painting things.

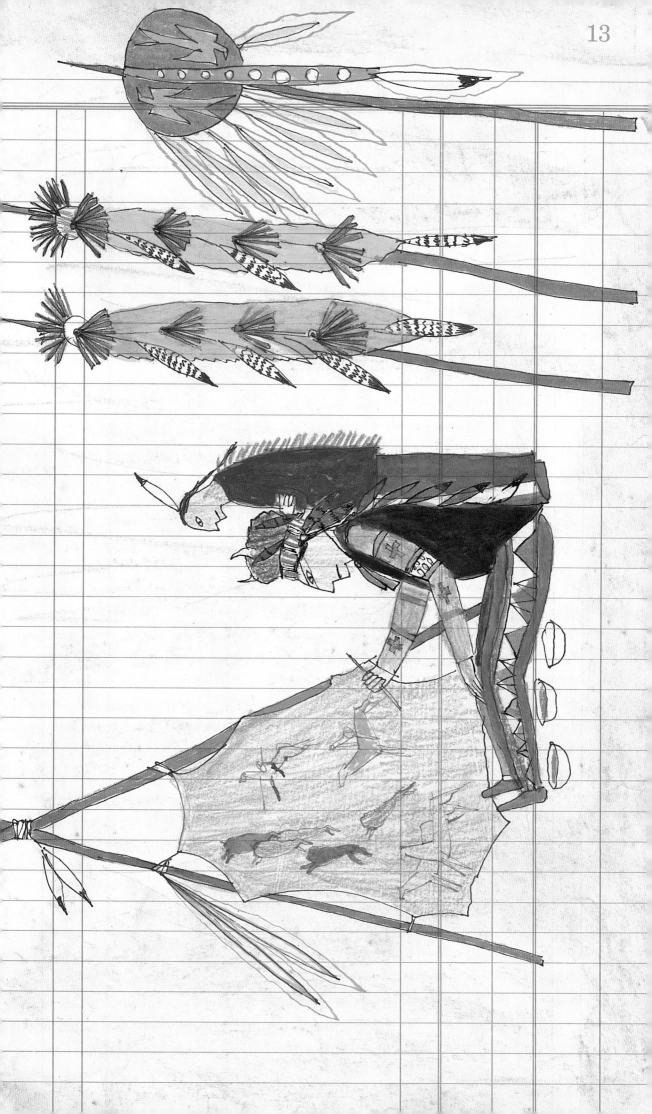

14

Our village played ball games and everyone made bets.

The ball was cut from scraps of buckskin sewed with sinew,

and we carved our bats from ash wood. Our field was as long

as the whole camp, and sometimes fifty men were on a team.

They painted their bodies and their bats and wore only breechcloths

and moccasins. We boys rode up and down the field on our ponies,

shouting at the players.

We followed the huge herds of buffalo over the Plains, packing our tipis on pony drags and our other belongings on dogs. When our hunters had killed as many buffalo as we needed, the women tanned the hides and dried the meat for food. We children gathered berries while our mothers made pemmican from tallow, bone marrow, strips of meat, and chokecherries pounded together. I kept some pemmican in my parfleche and ate it on long trips and on cold snowy days when there was no game to be found.

One evening when many of our men were away on an expedition

and I was scouting on horseback, I heard a strange noise.

I jumped down and crept through the trees. I discovered a party

of our enemies, the Crow, with their tall stiff hair, preparing

themselves for battle to take revenge for a horse raid our braves

had made. Suddenly the war party got on their horses and

galloped toward me on the way to our camp. I could do nothing

but hide, squeezed between two trees.

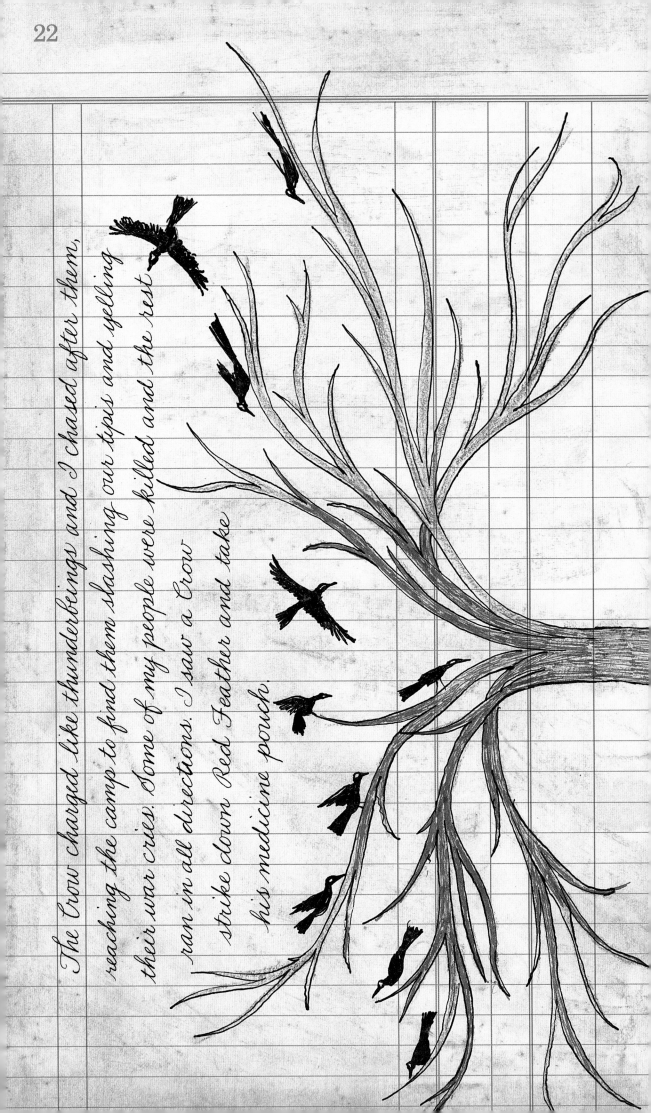

The Crow charged like thunderbeings and I chased after them,
reaching the camp to find them slashing our tipis and yelling
their war cries. Some of my people were killed and the rest
ran in all directions. I saw a Crow
strike down Red Feather and take
his medicine pouch.

I feared for my family and was full of much sadness. I climbed inside a hollow tree and remained very still. My presence did not even bother the winged ones. I asked the spirit of the tree to protect me.

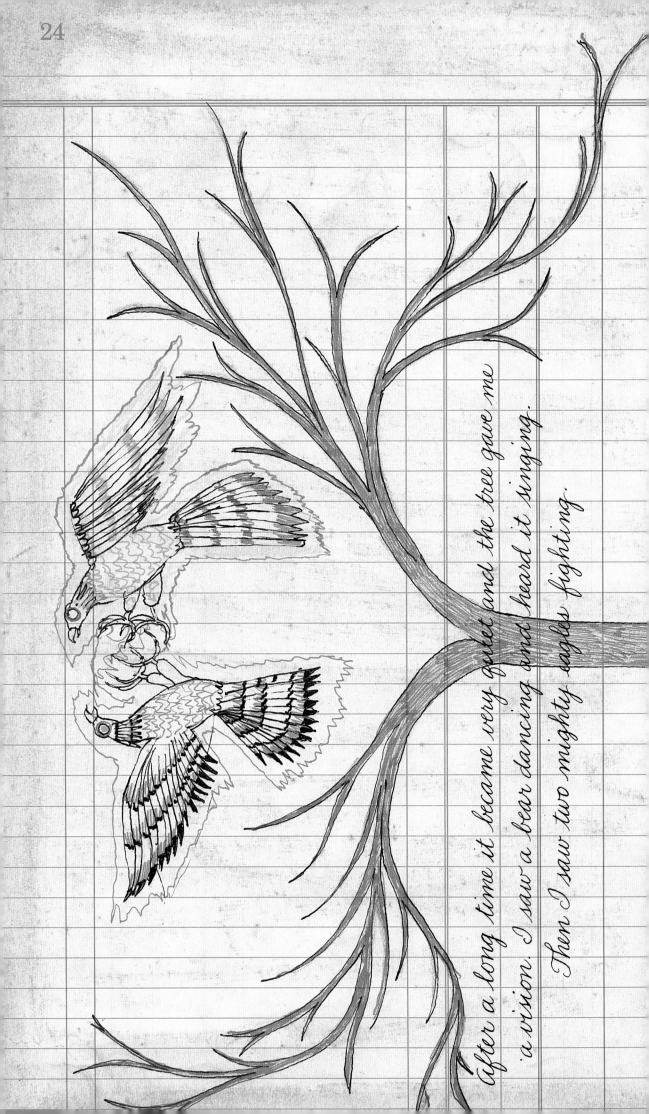

After a long time it became very quiet and the tree gave me a vision. I saw a bear dancing and heard it singing.

Then I saw two mighty eagles fighting.

Suddenly I too
became an eagle,
with blue feathered wings.
I soared into the sky
and disappeared.

When the sky became light I left the tree and ran into the hills

far away from our camp. I climbed higher and higher until I saw

an eagle's nest with three small eagles in it screeching for food.

As I scrambled up to the nest some of the rocks crumbled,

starting an earth fall. There was no way for me to go back down.

I fed the little birds some of the pemmican my mother had made

and their mother fed me. We drank rain water that collected in

a hollow place in the rock.

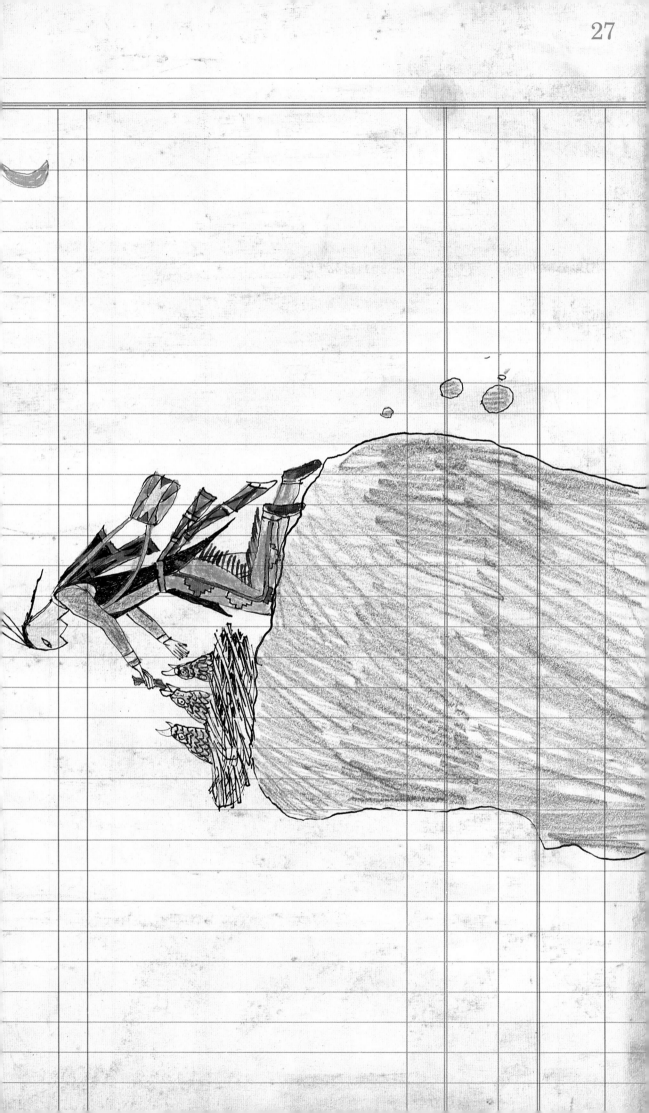

I stayed on the ledge until the Moon of Falling Leaves.

By that time my winged brothers had learned to fly and to hunt for their own food. I despaired of ever seeing my people and Two Painted Horse again. One day the parent eagles asked if they could help me find my parents. They lifted me gently with their strong claws and the others flew in front, making an upwards wind.

We glided down over the sharp crags to the foothills below.

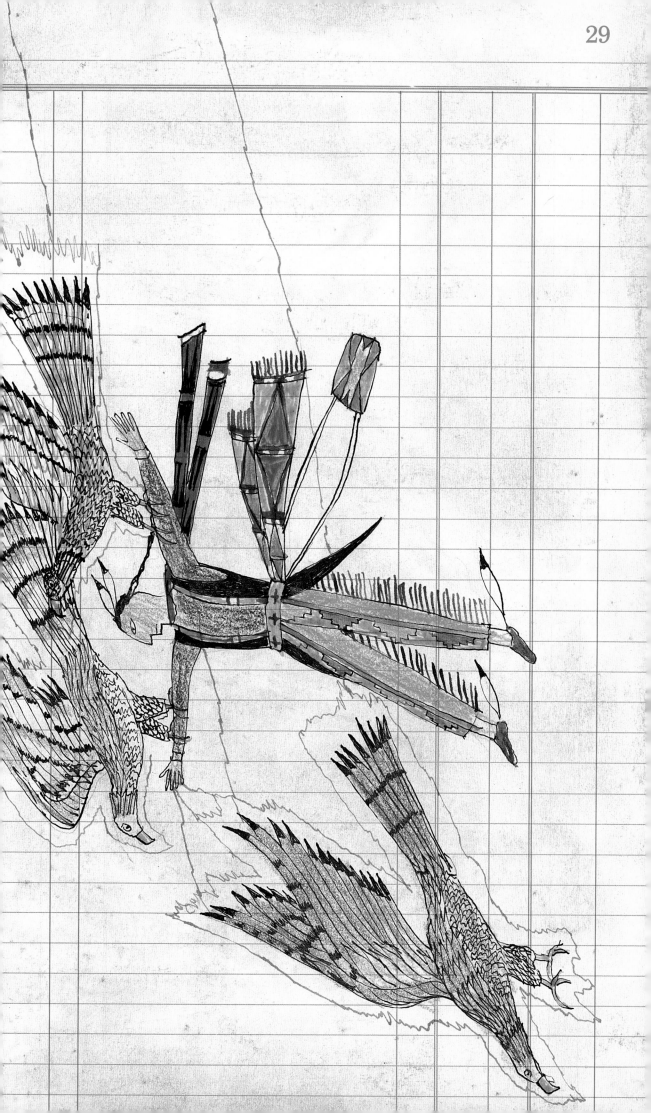

We flew far out over the Plains until we came near a camp.

I looked below and saw my father and mother and my Two Painted Horse.

The eagles set me down and I ran to my family. All our eyes were wet with happiness and my heart was full of thankfulness.

There was great joy and celebration.

I told of my vision and my time with the eagles.

My father was not surprised, for he knew that the eagles had great power.

After this I was called
Blue Eagle.

31

The first time I saw a white man I thought he was so pale.

He was a trapper who came to our land to hunt our animals and to trade with us.

I soon saw that the beaver skin on his chin was really his own hair.

From the hills Two Painted Horse and I spied on the trapper's mules.

I planned to capture them and take all the trapper's pelts.

After all, he had taken them from our land and had not traded us anything in return.

Mules are harder to steal than horses. They are slower and more stubborn. But the trapper's mules came willingly when they heard our calls. I was able to show my father how brave I was by stealing the white man's mules and his pelts while he set his traps.

I marked this coup on my coup stick.

Soon many more white men came rolling across our Plains in tipis on wheels. After a short time there was almost no room for us or for the four-leggeds. We had to travel great distances to find food.

I recalled Red Feather's warning and my dream about the battle of the eagles. My father told me that to survive these changes we must learn more about the white man but we must not become tangled in his bad ways. He told me to remember my dream and always to honor our ways and our Mother Earth.

The white man hunted all over our Plains and soon killed most of the buffalo. Then he was no longer content to cross our land with his iron road. He wanted to keep the land and the yellow metal that was in it. We made treaties to protect our hunting grounds. We were forced to move to a place called Reservation.

The white man broke the treaties. We went to war. We fought Long Hair Custer and defeated him. Soldiers swarmed into our hills with guns that fired many times without ceasing. Their guns were stronger than our trade guns.

There was much death.

42

A soldier came to my father and asked him to send me to a place called Carlisle Pennsylvania. The soldier promised to teach me the white man's language and his skills. He told my father that other children of head men were going to Carlisle. At first my father refused, but then he remembered my vision. With a heavy heart he said I could go. He wanted me to understand the strange rules and power of the white man.

I went with other children inside a long row of little houses sitting on the iron road. Suddenly the houses started to move and I thought they would fall over. The big boys told me the white men were taking us to the edge of the world and they would push us over the side. I was afraid but then I could see that they were testing me. They did not know where we were going either.

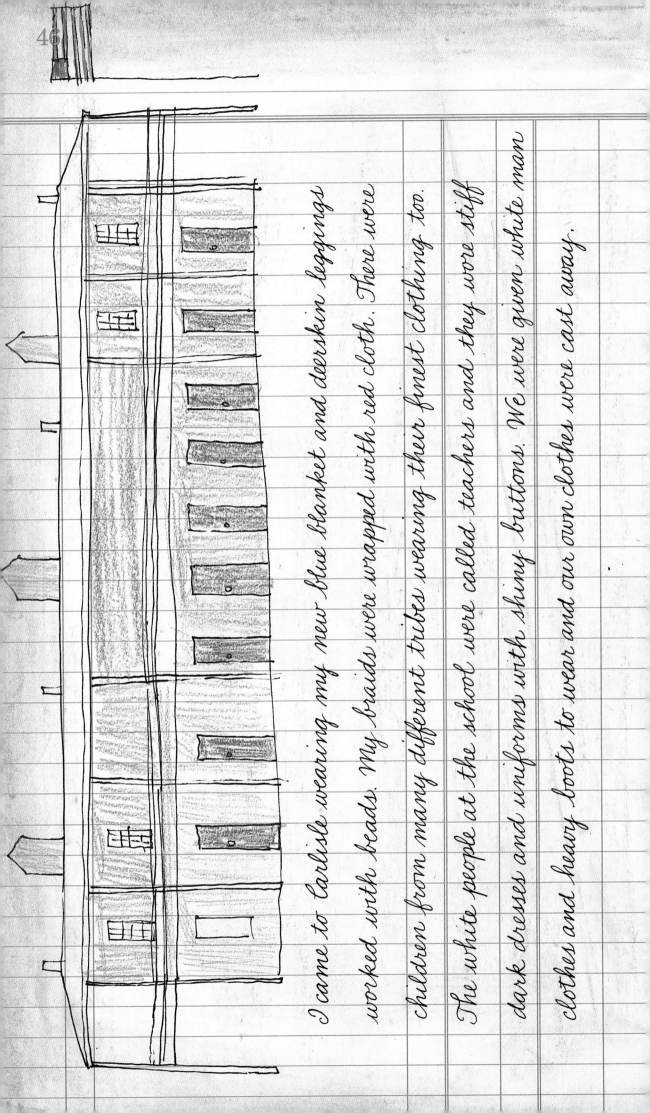

I came to Carlisle wearing my new blue blanket and deerskin leggings worked with beads. My braids were wrapped with red cloth. There were children from many different tribes wearing their finest clothing too.

The white people at the school were called teachers and they were stiff dark dresses and uniforms with shiny buttons. We were given white man clothes and heavy boots to wear and our own clothes were cast away.

48

The teachers cut off our long hair and made us baldheaded.

At first we thought our parents had been killed. It is our way to cut off our hair in mourning. But the teachers told us it was their way for young men to become educated. I did not know why I could not keep my hair to learn the ways of the white man.

49

Our teacher showed us marks on the blackboard that could be our new names. We each had to point to the one we wanted. It was not the Sioux way of earning a name. My friend Singing Bear who was Red Feather's granddaughter picked the name Julia for herself. She liked the sound of the English name Julia for herself. Thomas Blue Eagle. Tall Tree, a big Crow, became Henry.

We all learned reading, numbers, and geography. In the afternoon we boys did tinsmithing, printing, or carpentry, and the girls did sewing, cooking, or planting.

It made me think of Red Feather and his winter count. It made me think of my home and my four-legged friends and the winged ones.

Soon we all spoke the white man's language and we were forbidden to speak our own. We wrote our stories in English. We even made prayers to the white man's God, but I do not think he heard us.

My favorite part of school was when a teacher gave me this ledgerbook and color sticks to tell my story.

At night we had to wear long red suits that scratched our skin.

We slept on iron beds. It was very different from sleeping in my warm tipi under buffalo robes with Two Painted Horse nearby.

Each boy was allowed only one keepsake to remind him of his home.

I had the parfleche my mother had painted. In the belongings of Henry Tall Tree, I saw Red Feather's medicine pouch.

I knew I had to take that pouch back to my people.

We Carlisle boys loved to play football. The white man's football game was very different from our ball game. The ball was not round and everyone wore heavy woolen sweaters and spikey shoes.

When we played against other teams we always won because we were much faster. In one practice I was hit very hard by the bully Henry Tall Tree. He was wearing Red Feather's medicine pouch.

I jumped on him and he fell down. I got the football and the medicine pouch at the same time.

Tall Tree sneaked up on me one evening when we were camping out.

He was desperate to take back Red Feather's medicine pouch.

We fought for a long time and he stabbed me with something sharp.

I called out to him with power words and told him the medicine

pouch belonged to Singing Bear's grandfather. To my surprise,

Tall Tree dropped his weapon and slunk back toward the dormitory.

I kept the medicine pouch and went back to the school where

Singing Bear saw me bleeding.

Julia took the sacred things from Red Feather's medicine pouch.

She touched them to me and prayed to the Sacred Powers to heal me.

In a short time my wound closed and there was no more blood.

Then she called out to Tall Tree and told him that we must perform

a peace ceremony. Julia said that we three should be friends.

We were far away from our homes and this was a new time for all

of our peoples. I did not know that Red Feather's granddaughter

also knew healing ways. I had much regard for Julia Singing Bear.

Tall Tree brought tobacco in the town and I took a small pipe from Red Feather's medicine pouch. Julia lit the match and we all smoked the pipe. The smoke encircled up, lifting our prayers and thanks up to the Great Powers.

In this way Tall Tree became my brother and Julia my sister.

64

Now it has been six years and I will be going home. My family will

meet me with Two Painted Horse pulling their buggy. I will bring

Julia Singing Bear on my arm and we will return Red Feather's

medicine pouch to our people. I have learned the white man's ways,

as my father wished. I have learned his numbers and tools. I have

learned to tell my stories with the white man's words. I have also

learned that the white man does not see with the eyes in his heart

and that he does not hear our Mother Earth crying.

Wisdom comes to us in dreams.

When I am home, I will run on the Plains,
with Two Painted Horse, free like the wind.

I will cherish our Mother Earth and her gifts.

I will open my arms again to the Great Powers
and honor the dreams they send to me.

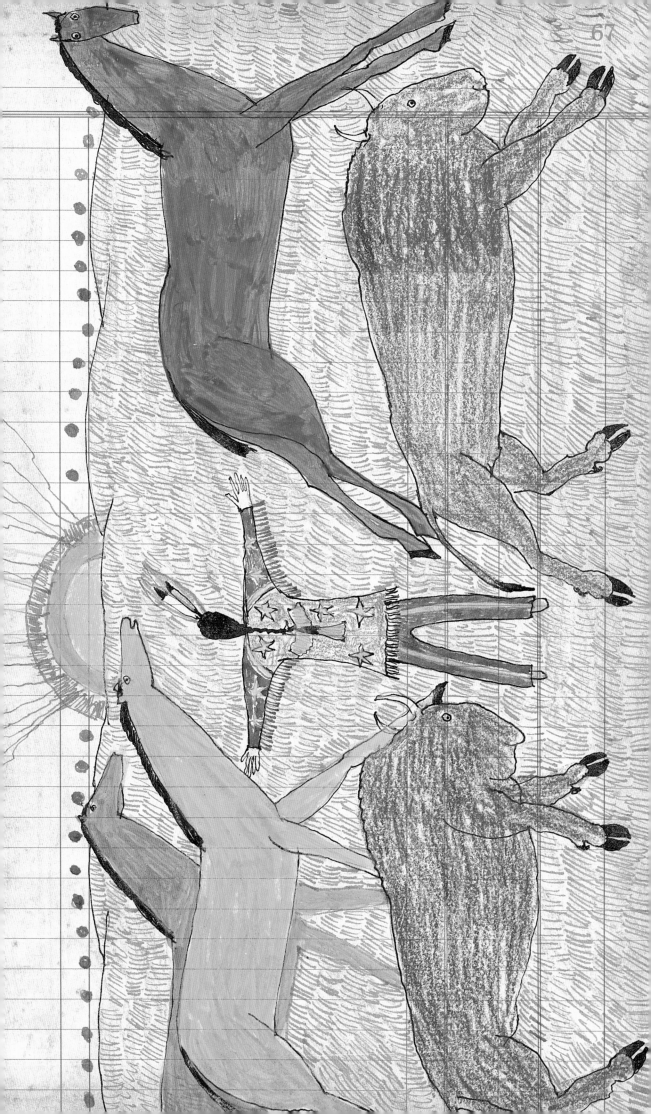

This book is dedicated to all the brave young Native Americans

who took that long, lonely journey into the white man's world

and studied at the Carlisle Indian School.

About Thomas Blue Eagle

Thomas Blue Eagle is a fictional character. Neither he nor any of the other persons depicted in his ledgerbook actually existed. Thomas Blue Eagle's ledgerbook supposes that the artist was able to tell his story in narrative form using both the white man's words and the Indians' picture stories. While no such ledgerbook has come to light, some may have been produced. Nevertheless, these imaginary drawings show events that might well have occurred in the life of a Sioux boy who attended school in the East to learn about the world of the white man. Thomas Blue Eagle's story is founded on historical facts and chronicles the clash of two completely different cultures in America toward the end of the last century.

Glossary

coup A successful stroke; one that captures the weapon or horse of an enemy, or an actual slap or series of slaps at the enemy. Each of these acts was counted as a coup.

head man It was more common for the Sioux to refer to their leaders as "head men" rather than as "chiefs."

parfleche A container made from hide (usually buffalo) which had been stripped of hair and dried stiff. These containers were often finely painted.

pony drag A kind of platform constructed of hide and bent willows stretched across wooden poles that were then attached to the sides of a pony or horse. Drags, also known as travois, were used to carry food and personal belongings over long distances.

Sioux Today the tribes formerly known as Sioux are known as the Lakota, if they live in the western part, and the Dakota, if they live in the eastern part of the Northern Plains.

thunderbeings Manifestations of the powers of the West, which are most obvious as thunder, lightning, thunder clouds, and summer storms originating in the West. Among some Plains tribes, these are sometimes personified as mythological thunderbirds, with lightning emanating from the clash of their beaks and the flash of their eyes and thunder from the flapping of their wings.

tipi A portable buffalo-hide dwelling in conical form, draped on tall wooden poles and joined near the top with wooden lodge pins. The seam was laced, and two flaps were left open for a smoke hole at the top and an entrance at the bottom.

About Pictographs and the Carlisle Indian School

The Carlisle Indian School did exist from 1879 to 1918. It was founded by Captain Richard Henry Pratt in a barracks that had been used by the army since the Revolutionary War. The Carlisle barracks is still used by the army today, housing its War College. The Indian school was designed specifically to teach young Indians the white man's skills in the civilized East, away from the reservations. As most of the children could not read or write in English and were forbidden to speak their own languages, at first they used slates and paper and coloring materials to communicate through word pictures.

Initially, the children recorded important events from their earlier lives, using the same traditional pictographic methods of their ancestors as they had observed their elders use in robe painting. Among the Plains Indians, pictographs were used in two distinctly different ways. Some were used as mnemonic devices to record historical events called winter counts and were painted on hides. Others were used in narratives, or stories, and were painted on robes, tipis, shields, and other objects. Stories told in pictographs normally read from right to left. Portions of figures often represented the whole. Cartoonlike, wavy lines were used to indicate dreams. Drawing was done freehand in pencil or ink, and the outline was then filled in with flat color. There was usually no attempt at perspective.

As the students learned to write in English, sometimes they added explanatory words to their picture stories. Almost from the inception of their studies at Carlisle, the children, both male and female, were exposed to the art forms favored by the white man. As a result, they rapidly developed different ways of drawing and eventually abandoned the pictographic style and the limitations that style placed on their artistic expression. Unfortunately, only a very few pictographic drawings made at Carlisle from the period 1879 through 1885 have been preserved, although many were created.

This book was inspired by the beautiful ledger drawings made by Plains Indians in the late 19th century contained in private collections and in various museums. It is in large part based on letters, pictographs, and documents from the Pratt papers located at the Beinecke Rare Book and Manuscript Library at Yale University in New Haven, Connecticut, and on journals, photographs, pictographic drawings on paper, and other materials located at the Cumberland County Historical Society in Carlisle, Pennsylvania.

About the Authors

Gay Matthaei is an interior designer who has specialized in historic restorations and art consultation. She is also a professional photographer. She and her twin sister, Jewel Grutman, have produced an award-winning art film entitled *Where Time is a River*. Mrs. Matthaei is the mother of three children and lives in New York City.

Jewel Grutman is an attorney and a photojournalist. She and her husband maintain an office in New York City but try cases all over the United States. They make their home in Greenwich, Connecticut.

About the Lakota Advisor

Arthur Amiotte provided invaluable cultural and historical insights. He is a Lakota artist, art historian, author, and educator who is well versed in the traditions of his tribe. His Lakota name is Good Eagle Center.

About the Artist

Adam Cvijanovic was born in Cambridge, Massachusetts, in 1960. His work has been featured in numerous group exhibitions throughout the United States. His latest one-man show was in 1993 at the Richard Anderson Gallery in New York City. His works are in several public collections including the Metropolitan Museum of Art, the Boston Museum of Fine Arts, the John and Mabel Ringling Museum in Sarasota, Florida, and the collections of the American Express Corporation and NYNEX Corporation. Mr. Cvijanovic lives and works in New York City.

Acknowledgements

The authors are indebted to Linda Witmer and her staff at the Cumberland County Historical Society for their kind assistance in providing from the archives artifacts produced at the Carlisle Indian School.

The Ledgerbook of Thomas Blue Eagle

First published in 1994 by Thomasson-Grant.

Reprinted 1997 by Lickle Publishing Inc.

Copyright © 1994

by Jewel H. Grutman and Gay Matthaei.

Illustrations by Adam Cvijanovic.

Calligraphy by Serelda Bedsole.

Lakota Consultant Arthur Amiotte.

Edited by Susie Shulman.

Design and production by Lisa Lytton-Smith.

Case stamping design courtesy of Boorum & Pease,

a division of Esselte Pendaflex Corporation.

Printed in China.

00 99 98 97 96 95 94 5 4 3 2

Library of Congress

Cataloging-in-Publication Data

Grutman, Jewel H.

The ledgerbook of Thomas Blue Eagle / story told by
Jewel H. Grutman and Gay Matthaei; illustrations by
Adam Cvijanovic.

p. cm.

ISBN 1-56566-063-3 (hardcover) :

1. Dakota Indians–History–Juvenile literature.

2. Dakota artists–Juvenile literature. 3. Dakota art–
Juvenile literature. 4. United States Indian School
(Carlisle, Pa.)–History–Juvenile literature. I. Matthaei,
Gay. II. Cvijanovic, Adam, 1960 - . III. Title.

E99.D1G77 1994

973'.04975–dc20   94–8966

                                                        CIP

                                                         AC

All inquiries should be directed to:

Lickle Publishing Inc

590 Madison Avenue 26th floor

New York, NY 10022

[212] 371-5444

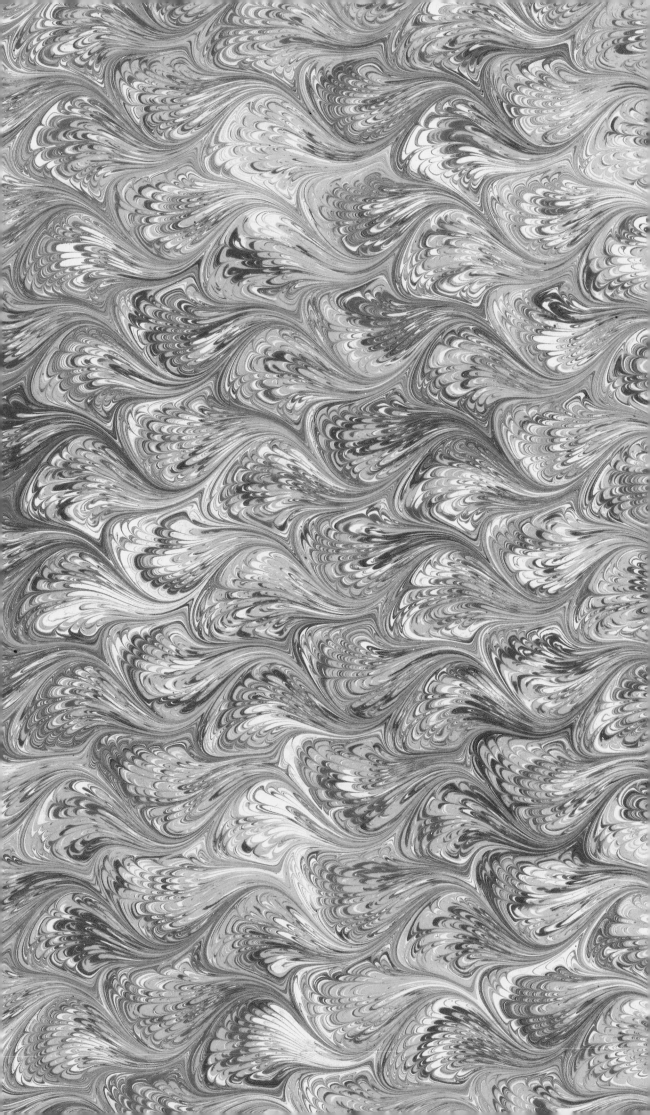

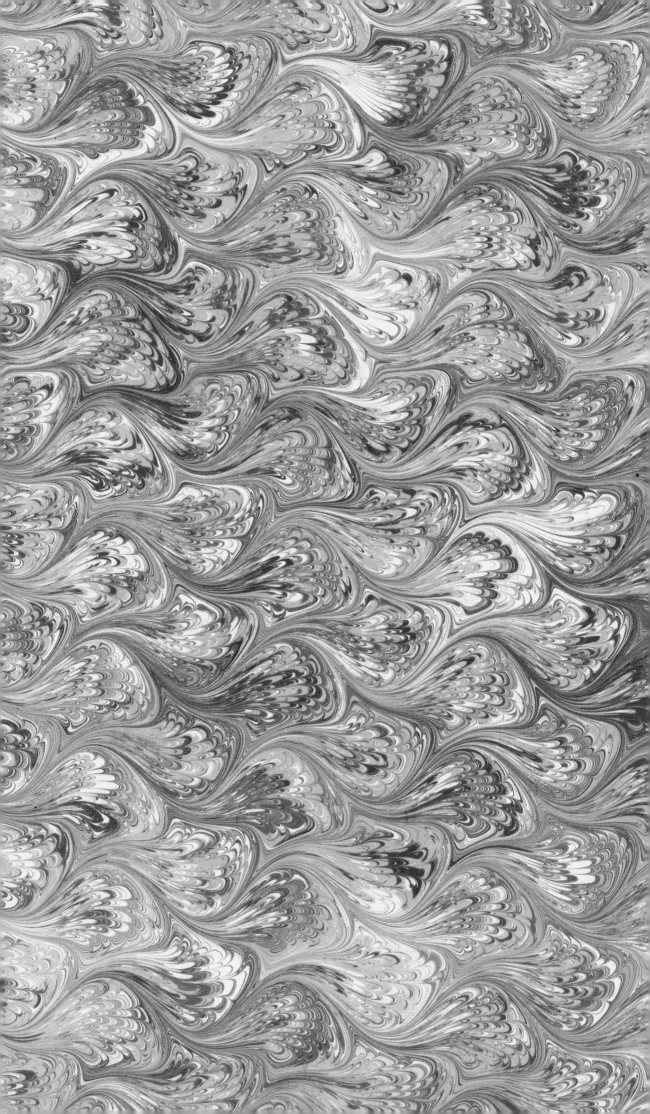